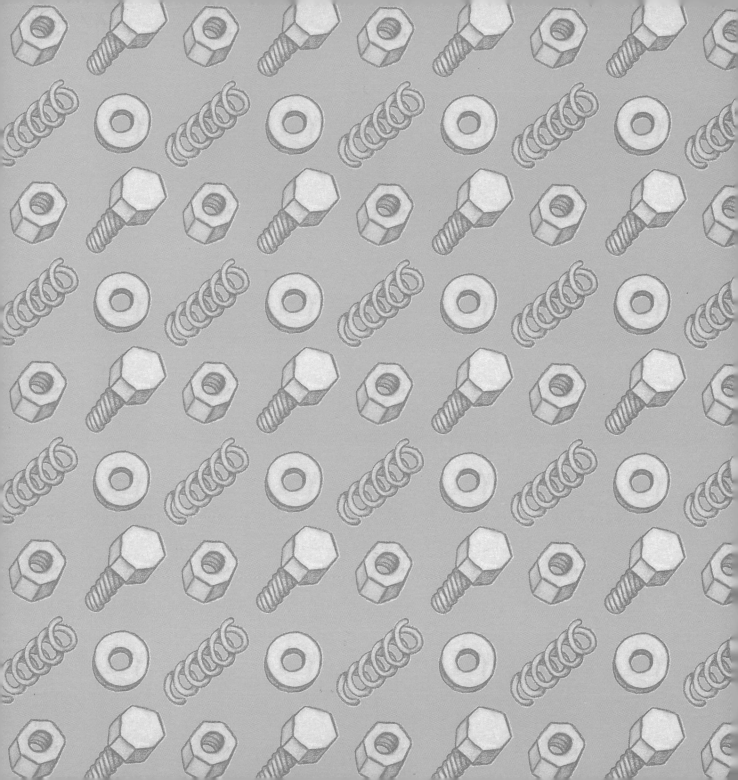

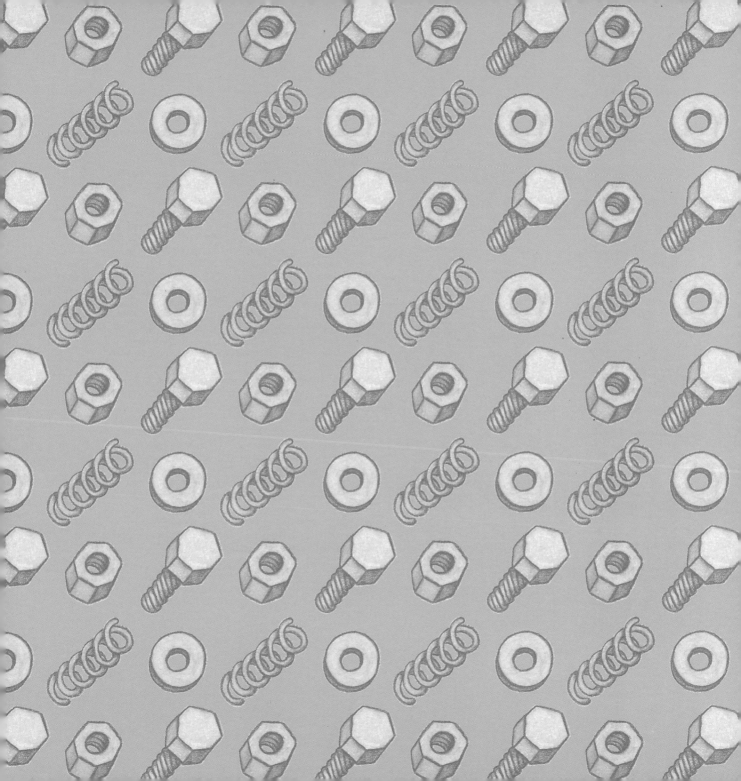

For Joseph: JB
For Ben: NS

Oxford University Press, Great Clarendon Street
Oxford OX2 6DP
Oxford New York
Athens Auckland Bangkok Bogota Buenos Aires
Calcutta Cape Town Chennai Dar es Salaam
Delhi Florence Hong Kong Istanbul Karachi
Kuala Lumpur Madrid Melbourne Mexico City
Mumbai Nairobi Paris Sao Paulo Singapore
Taipei Tokyo Toronto Warsaw

and associated companies in
Berlin Ibadan

Oxford is a trade mark of Oxford University Press

Illustration © Nick Sharratt 1991

Arrangement and Selection © Jill Bennett 1991

First published 1991
Reprinted 1993
First published in paperback 1993
Reprinted 1993 (twice), 1996, 1997 (twice), 1998
Paperback: ISBN 0–19–276114–5

A CIP Catalogue record for this book is available
from the British Library

Typeset by Pentacor PLC, High Wycombe, Bucks
Printed in China

Acknowledgements

The editor and publisher are grateful for permission to
include the following copyright material.

Dorothy Baruch, 'Funny the way different cars start' and
'Different bicycles' reprinted from *I Like Machinery* by
Dorothy Baruch (Harper, NY:1933). Copyright Dorothy
Baruch.**

Charles Causley, 'I Love My Darling Tractor' reprinted
from *Early In The Morning* (Viking Kestrel, 1986) by
permission of David Higham Associates Ltd.

Anne English, 'Washing Day' copyright Anne English,
reprinted from *Sit On the Roof and Holler*, ed Adrian
Rumble (Bell & Hyman).**

John Foster, 'Our Friend the Central Heating' reprinted
from *Things That Go*, ed. Tony Bradman (Blackie, 1989)
by permission of the author.

Robert Heidbreder, 'Little Robot' and 'Rockets'
reprinted from *Don't Eat Spiders*, poems © Robert
Heidbreder 1985, by permission of Oxford University
Press, Canada.

Barbara Ireson. 'U.F.O.' reprinted from *Spaceman,
Spaceman* (Transworld), by permission of the author.

Leland B Jacobs, 'The Underground Train' reprinted
from *Somewhere Always Far Away?*, © 1967 by Leland B
Jacobs, by permission of Henry Holt and Company, Inc.

Anne Le Roy, 'The New Phone' reprinted from *Big
Dipper*, ed. June Epstein et al (OUP Australia, 1981), by
permission of the author.

Marion Lines, 'Car Breakers', © Marion Lines, reprinted
from *Tower Blocks* by kind permission of Franklin
Watts, 96 Leonard Street, London EC2A 4RH.

Kit Wright, 'Cleaning Ladies' reprinted from *Hit Dog
And Other Poems* (Viking Kestrel, 1981) © Kit Wright
1981, by permission of Penguin Books Ltd.

We have tried to secure copyright permission prior to
publication but in the case of the entries marked ** this
has not been possible. If notified, the publisher will be
pleased to include full acknowledgement at the earliest
opportunity.

MACHINE POEMS

Collected by Jill Bennett
Illustrated by Nick Sharratt

OXFORD UNIVERSITY PRESS

I love my darling tractor

I love my darling tractor,
I love its merry din,
Its muscles made of iron and steel,
Its red and yellow skin.

I love to watch its wheels go round
However hard the day,
And from its bed inside the shed
It never thinks to stray.

It saves my arm, it saves my leg,
It saves my back from toil,
And it's merry as a skink when I give it a drink
Of water and diesel oil.

I love my darling tractor
As you can clearly see,
And so, the jolly farmer said,
Would you if you were me.

Charles Causley

Washing day

A washing machine
A sploshing machine
Splish, splash, splosh.
Whenever I use my washing machine
It splishes and splashes
All over the floor,
It splashes and sploshes
As far as the door.
I get into muddles
And step into puddles,
I don't think I'll use it
Any more.

Anne English

Funny the way different cars start

Funny the way
Different cars start.
Some with a chunk and a jerk,
Some with a cough and a puff of smoke
Out of the back,
Some with only a little click—
　　　　　　with hardly any noise.

Funny the way
Different cars run.
Some rattle and bang,
Some whirr,
Some knock and knock.
Some purr
And hummmmm
Smoothly on
　　　　　with hardly any noise.

Dorothy Baruch

The underground train

The underground train, the
    underground train,
If you'll permit me to explain,
Is like a busy beetle black
That scoots along a silver track;
And, whether it be night or day,
The beetle has to light its way,
Because the only place it's
    found
Is deep, deep, deep, deep under-
    ground.

Leland B. Jacobs

Cleaning ladies

Belly stuffed with dust and fluff,
    The Hoover moos and drones,
Grazing down on the carpet pasture:
    Cow with electric bones.

Up in the tree of a chair the cat
    Switches off its purr,
Stretches, blinks: a neat pink tongue
    Vacuum-cleans its fur.

Kit Wright

The new phone

We've got this new green phone, you see,
And all day long my friends call me,
And I just can't get on with things
Because it rings and rings and rings.

Anne LeRoy

Different bicycles

When I ride my bicycle
I pedal and pedal
Knees up, knees down.
Knees up, knees down.

But when the boy next door
Rides his.
It's whizz —
A chuck   a chuck —

And away
He's gone
With his
Knees steady-straight
In one place. . .
Because —
     His bicycle has
     A motor fastened on.

Dorothy Baruch

Little Robot

I'm a Little Robot,
    Wires make me talk.
I'm a Little Robot,
    Wires make me walk.
I'm a Little Robot,
    Wires bend my knees.
I'm a Little Robot,
    Wires make me sneeze.
            AAAACHOOOOOO!

I'm a Little Robot,
    Wires make me work.
So if you ever cross them,
    I'll probably go BERSERK!

ZOING ZOING BOINK!
ZOING ZOING BOINK!
ZING!

Robert Heidbreder

Car breakers

There's a graveyard in our street,
But it's not for putting people in;
The bodies they bury here
Are made of steel and paint and tin.

The people come and leave their wrecks
For crunching in the giant jaws
Of a great hungry car-machine,
That lives on bonnets, wheels and doors.

When I pass by the yard at night,
I sometimes think I hear a sound
Of ghostly horns that moan and whine,
Upon that metal-graveyard mound.

Marion Lines

Our friend the central heating

There's a monster in our house —
Our friend the central heating.
From the way its stomach rumbles,
Goodness knows what it's been eating!

It wakes us up at night-time
With its gurglings and its groanings,
Its clatterings and its clanging,
Its mutterings and moanings.

Mum says it lives on water,
In answer to my question.
I think that it must gulp it down
To get such indigestion!

John Foster

Rockets

Rockets flying out in space,
Rockets flying every place,
Rockets from Earth
      to Venus and Mars,
      to silver moons and shining stars,
Rockets to galaxies far away,
I think I'll build a rocket some day.
I'll fuel it first.
I'll fly it away.
I'll land in time for Christmas day,
On Pluto, Neptune, Saturn or Mars,
On a silver moon
Or a shining star.

Robert Heidbreder

U.F.O.

Hear that humming. . .
Spaceship's coming.

Watch that light. . .
It's shining bright.

Feel that air. . .
It's landing there.

Hear that roar. . .
Look at the door.

See the crew. . .
They're coming through!

Barbara Ireson

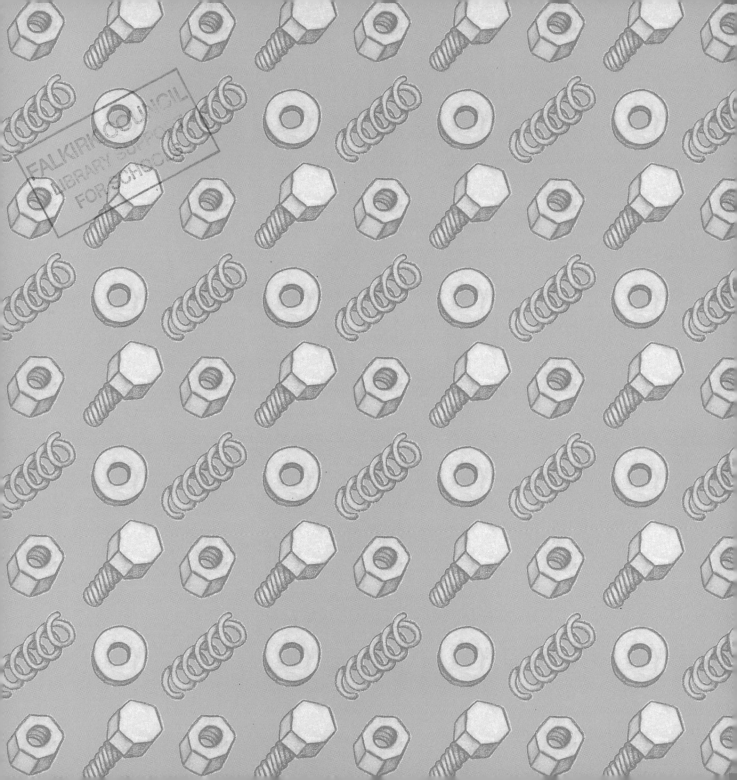

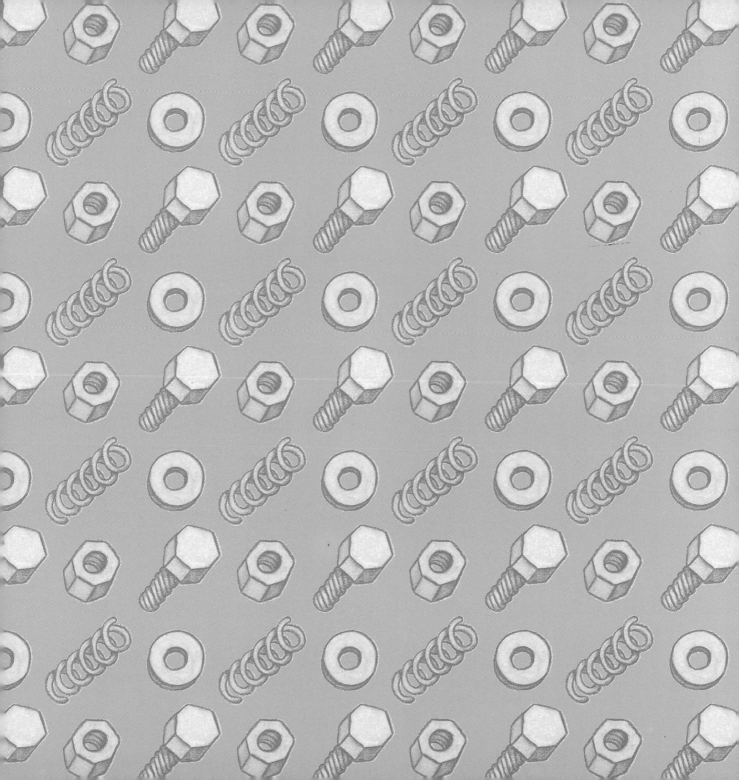